YOU CHOOSE BOOKS™

The Attack on Pearl Harbor

An Interactive History Adventure

by Allison Lassieur

Consultant:
David Aiken
Codirector, Pearl Harbor History Associates
Stratford, Connecticut

Capstone
press®

Mankato, Minnesota

You Choose Books are published by Capstone Press,
151 Good Counsel Drive, P.O. Box 669, Mankato, Minnesota 56002.
www.capstonepub.com

Books published by Capstone Press are manufactured with paper
containing at least 10 percent post-consumer waste.

Library of Congress Cataloging-in-Publication Data
Lassieur, Allison.
    The Attack on Pearl Harbor : an interactive history adventure / by Allison Lassieur.
    p. cm. — (You choose books)
    Summary: "Describes the attack on Pearl Harbor on December 7, 1941, as Japanese forces
surprised Americans at the U.S. military base, and explains the significance of the attack today.
The reader's choices reveal the historical details from the perspective of a Japanese pilot, a U.S.
sailor, and an American nurse" — Provided by publisher.
    Includes bibliographical references and index.
    ISBN-13: 978-1-4296-2010-9 (hardcover)   ISBN-13: 978-1-4296-2864-8 (softcover)
    ISBN-10: 1-4296-2010-2 (hardcover)   ISBN-10: 1-4296-2864-2 (softcover)
    1. Pearl Harbor (Hawaii), Attack on, 1941 — Juvenile literature. 2. Plot-your-own stories.
I. Title. II. Series.
D767.92.L38 2009
940.54'26693 — dc22
                                                                2007050513

Editorial Credits
Megan Schoeneberger, editor; Juliette Peters, set designer; Patrick D. Dentinger,
    book designer; Danielle Ceminsky, illustrator; Wanda Winch, photo
    researcher

Photo Credits
AP Images, 6; Courtesy of the National Park Service, USS Arizona Memorial,
39, 56, 78, 92; DVIC/PH3 (AW/SW) Jayme Pastoric, USN, 104; Getty Images
Inc./Hulton Archive/Keystone, 15, 19; Getty Images Inc./Hulton Archive/
MPI, 100; Getty Images Inc./Time Life Pictures/J. R. Eyerman, 94; Library of
Congress/Official U.S. Navy Photograph, 65, 86; National Archives and Records
Administration (NARA), 24, 28, 43, 84, 99; U.S. Naval Historical Center, cover,
10, 13, 17, 32, 40, 46, 48, 54, 62, 69, 75, 89; Zuma Press/Contra Costa Times/
photo courtesy Benjamin Smith, 96

Printed in the United States of America in Stevens Point, Wisconsin.
112011
006483

TABLE OF CONTENTS

ABOUT YOUR ADVENTURE

YOU are living in the early 1940s. Much of the world is at war. The United States hopes to stay out of it. But Americans keep a close eye on events in Europe and Japan. When efforts to keep the peace fail, whose side will you choose?

In this book, you'll explore how the choices people made meant the difference between life and death. The events you'll experience happened to real people.

Chapter One sets the scene. Then you choose which path to read. Follow the directions at the bottom of each page. The choices you make will change your outcome. After you finish one path, go back and read the others for new perspectives and more adventures.

YOU CHOOSE the path you take through history.

Leaders from Japan, Italy, and Germany signed an agreement to help each other in war.

A World at War

It is November 1941, and the world is at war. The fighting started in the 1930s, as powerful leaders dreamed of expanding their empires. Now, the leaders of Japan, Italy, and Germany have signed an agreement to help each other reach their goals. Together, these countries are called the Axis powers.

Most of the world is focused on fighting in Europe. In 1939, German ruler Adolf Hitler invaded Poland. Since then, Denmark, Norway, Luxembourg, and France have fallen to Germany.

7

Turn the page.

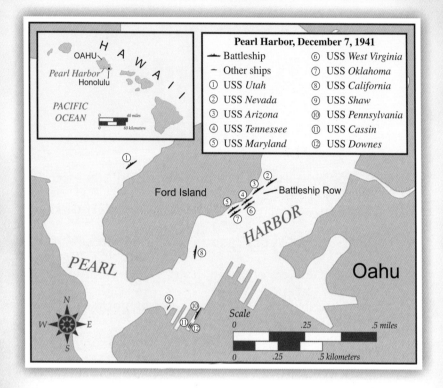

But before there was war in Europe, there was war in Asia. In Japan, military leaders want more land and more natural resources. In 1931, they took control of the Chinese region of Manchuria. In 1937, they attacked China. Now they occupy most of eastern China. Japanese leaders talk of bringing all of Asia under their control.

Meanwhile, the United States hopes to avoid fighting. Instead of soldiers, U.S. President Franklin D. Roosevelt sends money to Great Britain. He cuts off trade with Japan.

By early December 1941, the situation is desperate. War is coming. You just don't know when or where.

Then, on the morning of December 7, 1941, something happens that will change the course of the war. And you find yourself right in the middle of it.

✦ *To be a Japanese pilot, turn to page* **11**.

✦ *To be a U.S. Navy sailor, turn to page* **49**.

✦ *To be a U.S. Navy nurse stationed at the Pearl Harbor naval base, turn to page* **79**.

Admiral Isoroku Yamamoto planned the surprise attack on Pearl Harbor.

CHAPTER 2

Master of the Attack

As an officer in the Japanese Navy, you are one of the few who know about a top secret plan. For a few years, Admiral Isoroku Yamamoto and other leaders have been planning to attack the United States.

Yamamoto believes that only the United States has the power to stop Japan's expansion. But Japan lacks the resources to win a long, drawn-out war with America. A sudden, swift attack could destroy the U.S. naval fleet. While it recovered, America would be unable to join the war. Meanwhile, Japan could expand as it wants.

Turn the page.

Yamamoto's plan must be kept secret, even from your fellow pilots. If any hint of the attack gets out, the mission will fail.

In the late summer of 1941, you and your fellow pilots begin training. Fighter pilots practice air combat. Bomber pilots learn attack formations and how to drop torpedoes from very low levels. The torpedo planes fly so low that they almost touch the rooftops of nearby houses. The commanding officers study maps and models of Pearl Harbor and Oahu Island, where the United States keeps its fleet.

Under the cover of darkness on November 26, 1941, the attack fleet slips out of Tokyo Harbor. There are six aircraft carriers, *Akagi*, *Hiryu*, *Kaga*, *Shokaku*, *Soryu*, and *Zuikaku*. The fleet also includes battleships, cruisers, submarines, destroyers, and more than 400 airplanes. It is the largest strike force you've ever seen.

The Japanese aircraft carrier *Zuikaku* was part of the attack force headed to Pearl Harbor.

You are aboard the aircraft carrier *Akagi*. The strike force heads for the launch point 200 miles north of Oahu. In early December, Vice Admiral Chuichi Nagumo gathers everyone together. "I can now tell you what your mission is," he says. "We are on our way to Pearl Harbor in Hawaii. We will attack the American military base there. You are to destroy every battleship and aircraft carrier there."

Turn the page.

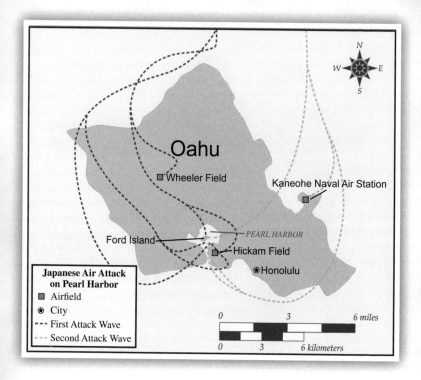

Japanese Air Attack on Pearl Harbor

■ Airfield
⊛ City
--- First Attack Wave
--- Second Attack Wave

Everyone starts talking at once. Nagumo quiets the crowd. "The attack will happen in two waves. The first group will attack the battleships and carriers. The second wave will attack what is left. Meanwhile, small submarines called midget subs will sneak into the harbor. We will attack the Americans from every side."

Japanese pilots received their orders before taking off from the aircraft carrier.

You're sure the attack will be a great moment for Japan. The world will finally understand your country's power. No matter what role you play in the attack, you will be making history.

→To join the first wave of the attack, turn to page 16.

→To join the second wave of pilots, turn to page 21.

The attack will begin at 6:00 in the morning on December 7. The night before, nobody sleeps. You talk for hours with the other pilots. Most of you are hopeful and proud of Japan for this bold attack. But some of the pilots are nervous. They say the sneak attack goes against the ancient Japanese customs of Samurai warriors. "The Samurai used to say, 'It does not do to slit the throat of a sleeping man,'" one pilot says. "It is wrong to attack without warning."

The next morning before you board your plane, you tie a white cloth called a *hachimaki* around your forehead. The cloth is marked with the symbol of the Rising Sun, just like on the Japanese flag. Written on the cloth are the Japanese words for "sure victory." Wearing the cloth means you are ready to die for your country.

Japanese planes wait to take off from an aircraft carrier the morning of December 7, 1941.

As you wait for your turn to take off, the ship pitches and rolls. You must wait for the winds to die down. Fifteen minutes later, you finally take off into the darkness.

Turn the page.

Your plane and more than 180 others roar south toward Pearl Harbor. As dawn spills over the horizon, all you see is the ocean below. Sunbeams shine through the clouds like the red beams on the Japanese Navy's flag.

When the clouds disappear, it becomes a beautiful, clear morning. You can see for miles. Finally, you glimpse land. Hawaii! It is a glorious sight. And there are no American fighters to greet you. Your attack force has surprised the Americans.

Commander Mitsuo Fuchida led the air attack on Pearl Harbor.

At 7:40, Commander Mitsuo Fuchida shoots a black flare. It is the signal to change into the attack formation. Nine minutes later, you hear a signal tapped over your radio. "*To, to, to,*" it says. Attack! The first planes begin dropping bombs on Wheeler Field. This fighter base is in the middle of the island of Oahu.

Turn the page.

At 7:51, you hear the signal "*To-ra, To-ra, To-ra.*" This signal tells you that the Americans have been taken by surprise.

By now, you're close enough to clearly see buildings, hangars, and other structures. A few pilots break away and head toward Hickam Field. Other pilots continue on to the harbor. Which direction do you go?

↠*To head toward Hickam Field, turn to page* **23***.***

↠*To continue to the harbor, turn to page* **24***.***

The first wave flies into the darkness, and the waiting begins. The ship is oddly quiet. Feeling restless, you make your way to the railing of the deck. There, you see a signal flag snapping in the wind. "The fate of the Empire rests on this battle. Let everyone do his duty," it says.

All around you, the planes are being readied for the takeoff of the second wave. You go to your plane and test the controls.

Finally, the carriers turn into the wind. At 7:15, your commander, Shigekazu Shimazaki, gives the order to take off. One by one, the 167 planes rise into the sky. You circle into formation and head south.

Turn the page.

At 7:49, you receive the radio signal telling you that the first wave has just begun its attack. A few minutes later, you get a second radio signal. It tells you the surprise attack was successful.

At about 8:45, you notice a low, dark cloud over the ocean. It is the smoke over Pearl Harbor. You move into attack formation. Some pilots head toward the harbor. Others are going to attack the airfields. If the planes are not destroyed, American pilots could fight back.

➤ To fly to the harbor, turn to page 37.

➤ To attack the airfields, turn to page 42.

You fly to Hickam Field on the southern edge of the harbor. Airplanes are lined up in neat rows. Perfect targets! This is going to be easier than you expected.

You fly low over the line of airplanes, looking for a good target. Planes ahead of you are dropping their bombs. Suddenly, an explosion clouds the air with black smoke. You can't see anything on the ground except smoke and fire. You are pretty sure you're close to a target. You could keep going and hope your bomb hits. But you don't want to waste your only bomb. Maybe you should circle around again. You have a split second to decide.

→ To pull out of your dive, turn to page 27.

→ To keep diving, turn to page 29.

American battleships were docked side by side in two neat rows.

You head for the harbor. As you approach, you see that your main targets, the carriers, are not there. Disappointed, you look for the battleships. They sit in two neat rows, completely undefended. You fly high in the sky and continue on toward the huge navy fleet.

➤ *To attack USS* Arizona, *go to page* **25**.

➤ *To attack USS* Tennessee, *turn to page* **32**.

You join the formation of planes heading toward *Arizona*. The battleship sits along the edge of Ford Island. On the deck, American sailors are gathered to raise the flag. They look confused as planes scream overhead. As bombs begin to fall, they scatter quickly. Soon it is your turn. You lock the target ship in your bombsight.

Before you can drop your bomb, an explosion in the front half of *Arizona* shakes the air. Flames cover the ship. A cloud of dark red smoke shoots up to the height of your plane. Tiny pieces of metal hit the planes ahead of you. In only a few seconds, *Arizona* is destroyed.

You still have a bomb to drop. You circle around again with your formation. As a group, you head toward *Nevada*, just beyond *Arizona*.

Turn the page.

Arizona's thick smoke makes your target hard to see. You can't tell if you're too close. If you don't drop your bomb at just the right time, you could miss. You don't want to waste your only bomb. Should you drop the bomb, or should you circle around again?

➤ *To make another pass, turn to page* **30**.

➤ *To drop the bomb, turn to page* **31**.

"Live now to fight later," you think, quickly pulling out of the dive. It's a good thing you did. Below, debris and smoke swirl in the air.

You climb safely higher and circle the airfield again. It's still hard to see through the smoke and flames. After three passes, you finally spot a few airplanes on the ground. You dive toward them.

"It's a clear shot," you think as you drop your bomb. The blast rips through the airfield as planes shatter into twisted metal. Gasoline from the engines catches fire, causing more explosions. American soldiers scurry below you, dodging flying metal and trying to put out the fires.

Turn the page.

Bombers destroyed airplanes on the ground at Pearl Harbor.

A signal comes over your radio announcing that the first attack is complete. You are to return to the carrier at once. As you climb into the air, you look at the destruction below. Dozens of fires rage out of control. Black smoke chokes the air. Admiral Yamamoto will be very pleased.

THE END

To follow another path, turn to page 9.
To read the conclusion, turn to page 101.

Circling around would give the Americans time to fire back. You must keep going. With a shout, you fly your plane straight into the cloud of smoke. Suddenly, your airplane shudders violently. You've been hit by something. The plane shakes again. You struggle with the controls.

Frantically, you look for somewhere to land. There's so much black smoke that you can't see the ground. Your plane goes into a steep dive. There's nothing you can do now. You're going to crash.

It is dishonorable to be captured. Instead, you decide to use your plane as a weapon. You're strangely calm as you guide your plane straight toward a group of buildings on the ground.

THE END

To follow another path, turn to page 9.
To read the conclusion, turn to page 101.

You'd rather be certain than sorry. You circle around once, then twice. On your third pass, you finally drop your bomb.

As you fly away, you look back to see whether your bomb hit. Instead of smoke and flames, all you see are ripples on the water. Your bomb missed. You curse your bad luck at wasting your only bomb.

At that moment, a signal comes over your radio to return to the carriers. There's nothing more you can do here. You turn your plane toward the open sea and fly back to the aircraft carrier. You're not looking forward to reporting your miss, but you're happy that the attack was successful.

THE END

To follow another path, turn to page 9.
To read the conclusion, turn to page 101.

You decide to take your chances. You drop the bomb and look to see if it hit the target. You see slight damage to *Nevada*. Your bomb hit, but it wasn't accurate enough to cause serious damage. You should have waited.

A signal comes over your radio to return to base. You fly high into the sky and follow the rest of the planes back to the carrier.

Turn to page **46**.

You search the harbor for *Tennessee*.
Then you see it, wedged between the shore
and another ship, USS *West Virginia*. There's
nowhere *Tennessee* can go.

West Virginia was struck by
up to nine torpedoes during
the attack.

Boom! You hear several explosions, and you fly around to get a better look. *West Virginia* and *Tennessee* are on fire. American sailors on the deck of *Tennessee* spray the flames with hoses.

Suddenly, something hits your plane. That's when you see several antiaircraft guns on *Tennessee* pointed at you. More bullets whiz past your plane.

➤*To keep attacking* Tennessee, *turn to page* **34**.

➤*To fly away, turn to page* **35**.

No American antiaircraft fire is going to stop you from your mission! You grit your teeth and make another run, dropping your bomb as you pass over *Tennessee*. You see it hit one of the turrets on the ship, but you can't tell if it exploded. Cursing, you circle your plane to get a better look.

Suddenly, your plane rocks violently. You've been hit! Those American gunners are better than you expected. They've shot right through your engine. Smoke billows from your airplane as it falls faster and faster toward the water. As your plane splashes violently into the water, you become one of the few Japanese casualties of the attack.

THE END

To follow another path, turn to page 9.
To read the conclusion, turn to page 101.

You didn't expect antiaircraft fire, and you don't want to be caught in it. You pull your plane higher, out of range of the American guns.

When you're above *Tennessee*, you drop your bomb. It somehow misses its target. The bomb falls into the water, exploding harmlessly.

Turn the page.

At that moment, you hear the signal to return to the carrier. You climb into the sky and look at the destruction below. You can't believe what you see. It looks as if all of the battleships are either destroyed or badly damaged. There is so much black smoke in the sky that you have trouble seeing. Flames cover many of the ships and Ford Island beyond.

"Returning to base," you reply. You're looking forward to reporting to Vice Admiral Nagumo. The attack was a bigger success than you ever imagined.

THE END

To follow another path, turn to page 9.
To read the conclusion, turn to page 101.

As you reach the harbor, you can make out a line of battleships along Ford Island. Smoke pours from some. Others spout waves of oil from their sides. You begin a steep dive toward the ships.

You catch USS *Pennsylvania* in your sight. But from the corner of your eye, you see USS *Nevada* moving slowly toward the channel out of Pearl Harbor. What luck! If you could sink *Nevada*, it would block the channel. No ships would be able to escape. You must decide quickly.

➤ *To go after* Nevada, *turn to page* **38**.

➤ *To continue attacking* Pennsylvania, *turn to page* **40**.

It is more important to block the harbor. You pull out of your dive. You and several other bombers swarm like bees above *Nevada*.

You swoop down again and release your bomb. At the same time, you pull back on the control stick. As you zoom upward, several bombs hit the ship. You hope that one of them was yours.

There's nothing more you can do. You soar overhead and watch other bombers go after the ship. After a few minutes, the ship turns slightly. It ends up on shore along the side of the channel. You didn't block the channel, but at least you damaged the ship.

You look at the harbor. Smoke and flames fill the air. There are piles of smoking, twisted metal where buildings and airplanes used to be. Several battleships are on fire, and a few were sunk.

Smoke poured from burning ships while *Oklahoma* slowly sank.

As you fly back to the carrier, a strange combination of pride and fear overcomes you. You are very proud that Japan was so successful. But you worry that the Americans will soon be waging war on Japan. There is no way to know what will happen then.

THE END

To follow another path, turn to page 9.
To read the conclusion, turn to page 101.

While other bombers go after *Nevada*, you continue your dive toward *Pennsylvania*. You fly nearer and nearer until the target nearly fills your sight. Just then, the ship bursts into flames. Another pilot has scored a direct hit.

Only one bomb hit *Pennsylvania*. It returned to service after just a few months.

As you look for a new target, a message comes through your radio. The attack is almost complete. All pilots should prepare to return to the carriers. But you still have a bomb, and you don't want to waste it. Maybe you could find another ship to attack. What do you do next?

→ To head toward another ship, turn to page **43**.

→ To return to the carrier, turn to page **46**.

You head toward Kaneohe Naval Air Station. There isn't much left. Below you, shattered planes and buildings cover the ground. Black smoke fills the air.

Suddenly, something hits your plane. Gunfire! To your astonishment, you see several American planes roaring toward you.

"Where did they come from?" you mutter as you frantically dodge and dive to avoid the gunfire. The planes must have survived the first attack. Several of your fellow pilots are shot down around you. For the first time, you wonder if you're going to survive the day. A U.S. plane speeds toward you, its guns blazing.

→ To shoot back, turn to page **44**.

→ To try to get away, turn to page **45**.

Fire caused the ammunition on *Shaw* to explode.

You head toward USS *Shaw*. It is docked near *Pennsylvania*. Several bombs have already hit *Shaw*, and it is burning. You dive toward the ship and drop your bomb. A massive blast rips through the ship. A huge ball of fire shoots into the air toward your plane. You watch as the entire ship and dock are swallowed in flames and smoke.

Turn to page 45.

You're not going to run! With a yell, you fire at the American plane. But you're not fast enough. Bullets rip through the cockpit, hitting you in several places. You scream in pain and let go of the controls as the cockpit fills with smoke. "This is it," you tell yourself. At least you were part of the successful attack. Japan will be proud of you, even if you don't make it back home.

THE END

To follow another path, turn to page 9.
To read the conclusion, turn to page 101.

As you quickly pull your plane out of danger, you receive the signal to return to the carriers. You and several other pilots head back to the aircraft carriers.

As you fly away, you take one last look at Pearl Harbor. Although a few ships still float in the harbor, most of them are badly damaged. The airfields on the island are almost destroyed. Many buildings, including machine shops, ammunition buildings, and storage buildings, are flattened. It will take months, maybe years, for the U.S. Navy to recover.

Turn the page.

You arrive safely back on your ship, tired but happy. You and the other pilots report on the attack. All of the pilots, including you, are eager to return for a third attack. Perhaps you could find the U.S. aircraft carriers.

Vice Admiral Nagumo is disturbed that there were no aircraft carriers at Pearl Harbor. He is worried that the U.S. carriers will find the Japanese attack force.

Vice Admiral Chuichi Nagumo was in charge of the attack force against Pearl Harbor.

Finally, Nagumo makes a decision. "There will be no more attacks," he says.

You can't believe it. You stare in amazement as Nagumo continues.

"It is too dangerous," Nagumo says. "We have achieved success here. We took the Americans by surprise and destroyed their navy. Our mission is complete, and it is time to return to Japan."

When you and the rest of the attack force arrive in Tokyo, you are welcomed as heroes for your bravery. That makes you happy. But the Americans have declared war on Japan. You'll be seeing them in battle again.

THE END

To follow another path, turn to page 9.
To read the conclusion, turn to page 101.

Arizona served in the Pacific during the 1930s and came to Pearl Harbor in 1940.

CHAPTER 3

Caught by Surprise

It is late 1941, and you are a young navy sailor, fresh from basic training. You're ready to serve your country, but you're nervous. Every day, you hear frightening rumors. Some people say Adolf Hitler will invade the United States. Others say that could never happen. Everyone is restless and uneasy. You don't know how long the United States can stay out of the war.

You are assigned to *Arizona* in Pearl Harbor. An assignment in Hawaii is a dream job, and you feel lucky. The weather is always mild. When you're not on duty, you and your friends spend time outdoors. You hike in the lush forests of Oahu or swim in the clear blue ocean.

Turn the page.

You live on the battleship in a room below the deck with several other sailors. You wake up early on Sunday, December 7. Sunday is your day to relax. You don't have any duties, so you and some of your buddies have requested shore leave this morning. They want to spend the day on the beach, and it sounds like fun. But you are feeling a bit lazy. Staying on board and relaxing also seems like a good idea.

→ To get up and join your friends, go to page **51**.

→ To stay in your room and relax, turn to page **53**.

If you're going to go ashore, you'd better get up now and get some breakfast. You dress quickly and make your way to the mess hall. It's not too crowded, and you easily find your friends.

"Looks like another gorgeous Sunday," you say as you sit down.

"You bet," your friend Bob answers, his mouth full of food. "Just think, a whole day off!"

While you discuss your plans for the day, another sailor sits down with you. "Hey, did you guys hear about the submarine they saw near the harbor?" he says.

"You mean an enemy sub?" you ask.

"Yeah, Japanese, I think," the sailor replies.

Turn the page.

"Oh, I don't believe it," your friend Tom says. "There's no way a Japanese sub could get here. The harbor is crawling with navy ships!"

After breakfast, you and your buddies go to the upper deck to watch the flag-raising ceremony. In the distance, you see a large group of airplanes flying toward the harbor.

"Who is that?" you ask.

"It's probably the bomber pilots that are supposed to come back today," Bob replies.

"Those guys are flying really low," Tom says.

Suddenly, an explosion rocks the ship. You don't know what's going on or what to do next.

→ To run to find an officer, turn to page 54.

→ To run to the railing to see what happened, turn to page 56.

Maybe you'll go to shore later, but for now, you decide to stay in your room. Your roommates are already gone. It's quiet for once, and you're going to enjoy it while you can. You prop yourself up and grab a book.

After a while, you hear the navy band playing "Stars and Stripes" on the deck above you. It must be about 8:00, time to raise the flag. You decide to get dressed.

Suddenly, the ship shudders. You hear a thud and shouts from the upper decks. You rush into the hallway. A sailor runs past, shouting, "We're under attack!"

You have no idea what to do. Your commanding officer is nowhere to be seen.

➤ To try to find an officer to get orders, turn to page 54.

➤ To go to your battle station, turn to page 64.

You and several others run toward the officers' quarters, hoping for news. Black smoke fills the air. The smell of burning oil and metal stings your nose.

You see Rear Admiral Isaac Kidd, the commander, running toward you. "Get to your battle stations!" he shouts. "Japan has attacked! This is not a drill!" Then he heads for the signal bridge.

Rear Admiral Isaac C. Kidd became the commander of *Arizona* in 1938.

Bombs rain down from above. You race to the ammunition storage area. It's your job to make sure the guns have enough ammunition to return fire. As you turn a corner, you nearly trip over a sailor lying on the floor. He's out cold.

You need to get to your battle station fast. But you want to help the injured sailor.

→ To continue to your battle station, turn to page **64**.

→ To try to help the injured sailor, turn to page **65**.

When you get to the railing, all you see is the airplanes filling the sky. Each plane is marked with a red circle. It's the Japanese symbol of the Rising Sun. Meatballs, you and your buddies call the symbols. You never thought you'd see Japanese planes flying over Pearl Harbor.

The Rising Sun is a symbol of Japan. The symbol was painted on Japanese planes.

People run and yell as the Japanese planes whiz past. Then another explosion rocks the ship. You grab hold of the railing to keep from being thrown overboard. Several men flip over the railing, screaming as they fall. At that moment, you hear a voice over the loudspeaker shout, "To your battle stations! This is not a drill!" You start to run to your battle station below the deck. But then you hear cries for help coming from the sailors in the water.

➤ If you stay to help the sailors who fell overboard, turn to page 58.

➤ If you obey orders and head to your battle station, turn to page 64.

You have to try to help these guys in the water. You haul a rope to the railing and throw it to the nearest man.

"Grab it!" you shout. With all your strength, you pull the man from the water. "Thanks," he gasps. He claps you on the back and runs off.

You wish you could help the others, but they're too far away. You climb down the nearest hatch and run through the passageway. You join a group of sailors running in the same direction. Suddenly, the ship shakes. The lights go out.

When the emergency lights flicker on, you see water rushing toward you. "Quick, open that other hatch," you say.

"It's jammed," another man answers. The water is rising fast. What do you do?

➤ To go back the way you came, go to page **59**.

➤ To try opening the hatch, turn to page **60**.

"Follow me!" You lead the men back down the way you came. The water is up to your waist now, and it's getting hard to walk.

Suddenly, the ship shakes violently. You hear several thuds from above you, and then a loud hissing noise. A rush of hot wind blows past your face. A ball of flame roars down the passageway. It's the last thing you'll ever see. You and hundreds of other young men burn to death aboard *Arizona*.

THE END

To follow another path, turn to page 9.
To read the conclusion, turn to page 101.

Another man, an officer, quiets the group. "If we can loosen the latches, we can get out of here," he says. "There's one set at the top of the hatch and one set at the bottom."

With a deep breath, you dive into the waist-deep water. You feel your way around the hatch until you find the latches. You pull several times, and they move a little. You come up for air.

"I've almost got them," you say. You dive again and pull. The latches give way! You come up again and shout to everyone, "Open the hatch before the water pressure is too high!"

Seven pairs of hands pull the hatch open. Water drains into the hatch as you and the other men climb through the hatch to safety.

On deck, bodies lie everywhere. Smoke chokes the air. The ship leans so far to one side that you can hardly believe that it hasn't sunk. Several men abandon the ship, jumping into the water. But if you stay on board, you might be able to save other sailors. What do you do next?

➻To abandon the ship, turn to page **62**.

➻To stay on board, turn to page **63**.

The wreckage of USS *Arizona* burned for several days after the attack.

"We've got to abandon ship," you shout. You and the other men quickly drop a lifeboat into the water and climb into it. As you paddle away, a huge explosion seems to blow open the sky. *Arizona* is lost in flames and black smoke. In just a few minutes, the ship sinks.

You've survived the sinking of *Arizona*. All you can do now is wait for a rescue boat.

THE END

To follow another path, turn to page 9.
To read the conclusion, turn to page 101.

"I'm going to stay here and help these guys," you say to the others. You start checking the bodies for signs of life. Most of the men are badly burned. Some of them have deep cuts from metal debris. None of them are alive.

You stand up and head toward another part of the deck. Just then, another explosion shakes the deck and throws you forward. You feel a blast of hot wind and see a huge firestorm coming at you. You cover your head as the flames reach you. But there is no escape. You are one of the 1,177 men from *Arizona* to die during the attack.

THE END

To follow another path, turn to page 9.
To read the conclusion, turn to page 101.

You rush toward your battle station. As you run, you see your friend Bob and grab his arm.

"Where are you going?" you yell over the roar of explosions, flames, and shouts.

"I heard an officer give the order to abandon ship!" he yells back. "I'm getting off this ship!"

A column of flames and smoke rises above the deck. You can feel the heat from the flames.

"Come with me!" Bob yells. "It's your only chance."

You hesitate. You have time to escape. But you don't feel right abandoning the ship without trying to fight back.

➤To continue to your battle station, turn to page 67.

➤To try to escape, turn to page 69.

You can't leave the man here, so you grab him by the feet and try to drag him. Officers and other sailors run past you, leaping over the man as more bombs explode above you.

You hear a loud blast, and *Arizona* shakes violently. Flames roar through the ship. You have to get away from them, and you can't drag the injured man with you. You take a deep breath and jump overboard.

Black smoke poured from burning battleships during the attack.

A shout rings out from a small rescue boat nearby. A man reaches down and grabs your badly burned arm. "We'll get you fixed up, sailor," he says as he gently hauls you into the boat.

Eventually, the rescue boat lands on shore. You're taken to the hospital on Ford Island. Stretchers fill the parking lot, holding hundreds of wounded. There are only a few doctors and nurses examining the injured.

Hours later, you're put into a hospital bed, where you stay for several weeks. Your burns are bad, and you lost three fingers. When you are released, you are discharged from the military. You go back to your hometown to wait out the rest of the war.

THE END

To follow another path, turn to page 9.
To read the conclusion, turn to page 101.

No, you have to stay with the ship. "Go on, and good luck!" you say to Bob. He gives you a surprised look and then disappears into the smoke. You hope he makes it.

You turn and run. Soon you reach the storage area. Officers scream orders as you try to get the ammunition out and up to the deck. People run and shout, and it's hard to know exactly what to do. But you're strangely calm. You signed up to fight for America, and this is your chance.

Turn the page.

Suddenly, a bomb lands on the front of the ship, rocking it so hard that everyone falls to the deck. Then, a deafening blast fills the air. The fire instantly roars through the area.

You see everything around you burst into flames. You don't realize at first that you're on fire too. The pain lasts only a few seconds. Then it's all over. You've given your life to defend the United States.

THE END

To follow another path, turn to page 9.
To read the conclusion, turn to page 101.

Oklahoma sank
next to *Maryland*.

You and Bob race to the deck. Bombs rip
through the ship as you run. When you get there,
you can't believe what you see. Flames and smoke
are everywhere. People are running, planes are
screaming overhead, and blasts fill the air.

Turn the page.

A huge explosion throws you high into the air. When you hit the deck, your leg crumples beneath you. You scream in pain and sink onto the deck. It is warm from the heat of the fires around you. You're covered in sweat, ashes, and blood. You don't see Bob anywhere.

You don't think you should stay here. But you're not sure you can make it off the boat. You try to stand, but the pain is too bad. You could crawl to the edge of the deck. Or you can stay here and hope someone rescues you.

➣ To wait to be rescued, go to page **71**.

➣ To abandon ship, turn to page **72**.

You think it's safer to stay here. You call out to several sailors running across the deck. Then your friend Tom appears out of the smoke. "I thought I heard your voice!" he yells. He picks you up and throws you over his shoulder. You almost faint from the pain. Tom carries you as fast as he can toward the railing. "There's a rescue boat out there," he shouts.

A huge explosion erupts around you, then another. The ship shakes violently, and Tom loses his balance. You both fall to the deck as a wall of fire roars toward you. There is no time to move. Even though the war has barely begun, for you, it's all over.

THE END

To follow another path, turn to page 9.
To read the conclusion, turn to page 101.

If you stay here, you'll die. You inch across the deck, groaning with pain as you drag your injured leg behind you. With a huge effort, you lift yourself over the railing and plunge into the water below.

The water is sticky with gasoline, oil, and blood, and soon you are too. Men are floating in the water all around you. Some of them are dead, burned so badly that you don't recognize them. A few, like you, are still alive. And still the bombs keep coming.

You feel yourself falling unconscious. "No!" you think, shaking yourself awake. If you pass out, you'll die.

Somewhere through the smoke, you think you hear voices calling. You could try to swim toward the voices. Or you can grab some debris and stay here, hoping someone will find you.

To try to swim, turn to page 74.

To grab something and hang on, turn to page 75.

You're pretty sure you can make it to the voices, so you start to swim. Pain instantly shoots up your leg. You struggle forward, trying not to faint. You can't see through the smoke.

The voices seem to be moving around, so you try to follow the sound. Just a little farther, and you'll be there. But you don't find anyone. You're very tired and in terrible pain. "I'll rest a few minutes, and then I'll try again," you think. With a sigh, you lie back in the water. Slowly, the pain goes away as you slip into unconsciousness and drown.

74

THE END

To follow another path, turn to page 9.
To read the conclusion, turn to page 101.

You grab a life preserver floating by and hang on tight. A few minutes later, rough hands grab you and pull you into a rescue boat.

"Am I going to make it?" you moan.

"Of course, sailor!" the man says. "You're going to be fine."

"Where are you taking me?" you ask. "Is anything left in the harbor?"

Rescuers in small boats were able to pull survivors from the water during the attack.

Turn the page.

The man frowns as he tucks a blanket around you. "Not much, from the looks of it," he says. "But you're alive, and that's what counts. We're taking you to *Solace*."

USS *Solace* is a hospital ship. It was not damaged in the attack. You'll be safe there.

You fall into unconsciousness. When you wake up, it's dark. You're in a soft, clean bed, and your wounds have been bandaged. You try to move, but your leg is in a heavy cast.

"Ah, you're awake," a nurse says, giving you a sip of water.

"*Arizona?*" you ask. "What happened to my ship?"

The nurse's eyes fill with tears. "Destroyed," she says. "The bombs hit the ammunition stores, which exploded. It tore the ship in two. You're very lucky to be alive." You lie back, stunned. The United States has no choice but to join in the war now.

After a few weeks in the hospital, you recover from your injuries. It's a good thing, because you've been itching to get to war since the attack.

The day you are released, you get orders to report to another ship, USS *Maryland*. This ship was only lightly damaged during the attack. Soon you'll be out to sea, a part of the U.S. forces in the South Pacific.

THE END

To follow another path, turn to page 9.
To read the conclusion, turn to page 101.

Beaches and warm weather attract many people to Hawaii.

CHAPTER 4

On the Shore

After finishing nursing school, you joined the military. You like the idea of being able to travel and see the world. You couldn't believe your luck when your first assignment was at a base in Hawaii.

Hawaii turns out to be as beautiful and interesting as you thought it would be. The only thing that spoils your enjoyment of your new home is talk of war. Today, though, war is far from your mind. It's a gorgeous Sunday morning, December 7. You have a rare day off.

Turn the page.

You're making coffee when you hear a strange noise. You look out your window and see a large fleet of planes flying fast and low over your house. "Someone should report those guys," you think. Pilots shouldn't disturb people on a Sunday. Then you notice the red sun symbol on the planes. "Those aren't our boys," you say out loud.

Before you have time to think, you hear the sound of bombs exploding in the distance. You run outside. The first columns of black smoke rise from the harbor.

Suddenly, people fill the streets. Shouts of "Attack!" echo through your neighborhood. You've got to get to the hospital. There will be wounded people, and every nurse will be needed.

You rush into your house and quickly change into your white nurse's uniform. Then you run back into the street, hoping you can find a ride to the hospital. A car screeches to a stop in front of you. It's one of your neighbors. He's a medic at one of the field hospitals.

"Please take me to the hospital!" you cry.

"Okay," the man replies. "But they also need help on the docks with the wounded men coming off the boats. I'm headed to the harbor."

You hesitate. You know they'll need you at the hospital. But you might be of help at the harbor too.

➺ To go to the hospital, turn to page 82.

➺ To go with the medic to the harbor, turn to page 84.

"I need to get to the hospital," you shout as you jump in the car. Your neighbor nods. It's not far to the hospital, but the drive seems to take forever. Smoke and the smell of burning debris fill the air.

At the hospital, you jump out of the car. "Good luck," you call to your neighbor as he speeds away toward the harbor. You can hear the loud rumble of planes overhead and the crash of bombs as they hit their targets. You run into the hospital.

"Thank goodness you're here!" says a doctor you've never met. "Many doctors and nurses are away at a meeting. We're short-staffed."

"What can I do?" you ask, looking around.

"Several first aid stations are being set up near the ships," he says, looking worried. "They're going to fix up the less serious injuries. But the badly injured patients will need to come here. We need people to drive them."

It seems that you're needed everywhere. You can be useful either at the shore or in the hospital. Which do you decide to do?

83

✦ To volunteer to drive the injured, turn to page **86**.

✦ To stay at the hospital, turn to page **94**.

It only takes you a few minutes to get to the shore. The medic gives you some first aid supplies and then disappears into the smoke.

You look around, unsure of where to go. The noise is deafening. Shouts, screams, and explosions fill the air. The sky is black with smoke. You duck as debris and bits of flaming metal fly through the air.

Crews attempted to put out the fires on *West Virginia* and other ships in the harbor.

A giant explosion suddenly rips through the harbor, violently shaking the ground. You fall to the ground just as an enormous ball of fire shoots from *Arizona*. Smoke and fire consume the battleship. Several other ships have caught fire and are burning.

You finally tear yourself away from the horrible sight of the destroyed ship and run to the water. Hundreds of men are floating in the water. On shore, several people are trying to get the injured to safety. You quickly begin helping the injured out of the filthy water. Many of them are badly burned. Breaking open your first aid supplies, you try to do what you can. Soon, you see a ship on the water. It's *Solace*, a hospital ship.

➻ To help the doctors aboard Solace, *turn to page* **90**.

➻ To stay on the shore, *turn to page* **92**.

"I can drive the injured," you offer. "We can't help anyone if they can't get to the hospital."

The doctor nods and hands you the keys to a maintenance truck. You jump in and race toward the harbor. Japanese planes fill the sky above the battleships. Bombs come down like hail. People are running everywhere. The smoke makes the sky as dark as night.

USS *California* was badly damaged in the attack.

You arrive at the water's edge just as rescue workers are pulling victims from the harbor. You and two medics carefully lay several injured men in the back of the truck. Without a word, you speed to the hospital. There you help carry the injured to the emergency room. Then you quickly drive back to the harbor.

You make several runs to and from the hospital. The back of the truck is filled with injured men. As you load one badly burned man into the truck, he weakly grabs your hand.

"What . . . where . . ." he whispers.

"You're being taken to the hospital, sailor," you say. "The Japanese have attacked Pearl Harbor."

Turn the page.

The man groans. "I was in the gun turrets when the bombs hit," he says. "Next thing I knew, I was in the water. Fire everywhere. Don't know how I got there."

"Try to relax," you say. You try not to look at his severely burned hands and face. Instead, you smile reassuringly. "We're going to get you fixed right up."

As you leave for the hospital, you notice a Japanese plane flying very low overhead. You quickly swerve down a side street. A few seconds later, you hear a huge explosion. There's a plume of fire and smoke near the hospital.

When you get to the hospital, you're relieved to see that the bomb didn't hit the building. But a nearby building was destroyed. The wreckage of a Japanese plane burns in front of the building.

This Japanese plane crashed near Pearl Harbor during the attack.

"What happened?" you call to a soldier running across the parking lot.

"He crashed!" he answers. "We're lucky he didn't hit the hospital!"

You agree. If he'd hit the hospital . . . you don't want to think about it. Right now, you've got a job to do. The hospital is going to need every pair of hands available.

Turn to page 94.

Quickly, you board a small rescue boat from *Solace*. It's heading toward *Arizona* to rescue the injured there. When you arrive, you and the other rescuers climb aboard. You don't have a lot of time. The ship is on fire, and the smoke is so thick that you can't breathe. You can feel the heat of the metal deck through your shoes.

"Come with me," one of the rescuers calls to you. You run toward two sailors who are lying facedown on the deck. All around you, sailors are abandoning ship, but you're not going anywhere. You and the other rescuers find several injured men and carry them to the rescue boat.

Back at *Solace*, you help unload the injured. Before you're finished, a doctor comes up to you.

"Nurses are needed at the hospital," he says. "They're shorthanded."

"But we're shorthanded here too," you reply. Now you're not sure what to do.

➤To go back to the hospital, turn to page **94**.

➤To stay on *Solace*, turn to page **98**.

You can be of more use here on shore. There is blood, oil, and gasoline everywhere. The attack finally ends. But your work is just starting.

As the men are rescued from the filthy, oily water, you bandage their wounds and try to make them comfortable. Trucks, jeeps, and ambulances come and go. You help load the injured men for their trip to the hospital.

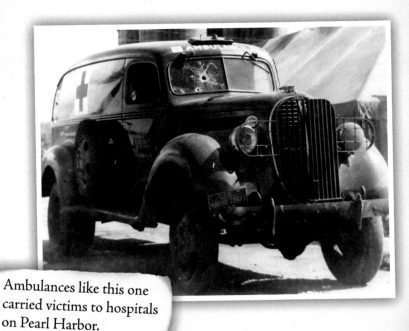

Ambulances like this one carried victims to hospitals on Pearl Harbor.

Men have been hit by bits of metal and other debris. Some are horribly burned and injured. But sailors who were wearing long pants and shirts have only minor burns. Those wearing shorts and T-shirts have worse injuries.

Over the next few days, you help care for hundreds of people injured in the attack. You're too busy working to pay much attention when Congress declares war on December 8.

About a week after the attack, you get new orders for duty on USS *President Coolidge*. You will care for patients who are being transported from other places. You wonder what will happen next. No one knows how the war will turn out, but you are determined to do whatever you can to help.

THE END

To follow another path, turn to page 9.
To read the conclusion, turn to page 101.

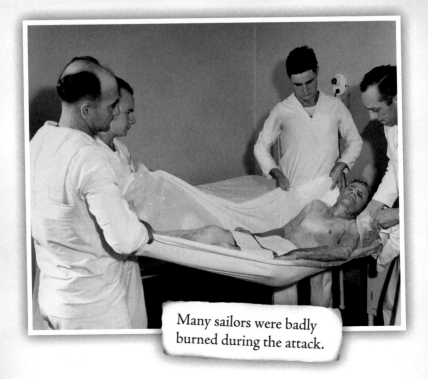

Many sailors were badly burned during the attack.

The hospital overflows with injured men. You barely have time to wash your hands before you're called to help. Most of the men have been terribly burned by the fires on the ships. You and the other nurses bandage their wounds and give them medicine to ease the pain. Cots are quickly set up in the hallways, and soon they are filled too.

Some time later, you notice that the number of injured coming in is slowing down. "What's going on?" you ask a passing soldier.

"Attack is long over," he replies tiredly. "They came in two waves. The first one pretty much destroyed our battleships and planes. We managed to get a few shots in when they came back an hour later."

You spend the rest of the day caring for the injured and the dying. As you wash the face of one young sailor, he wakes up and looks at you. "Where are Jim and Billy?" he asks.

"I don't know," you're forced to say. "What happened to you?"

Turn the page.

The sailor looks away. "We were on *Oklahoma*," he says. "Never saw so much smoke and fire in my life. Jim and Billy were trapped below deck. Some other guys and I tried to open the hatch, but it wouldn't budge. Then everything went dark."

"Both your legs are broken, but you'll be fine," you tell him.

Many of the sailors at Pearl Harbor were young men.

The man's eyes fill with tears. As you leave him, you hope that he'll find his friends someday. But you know he probably won't.

By nightfall, you're exhausted. After a few hours of rest, you're back at work. Someone turns on a radio. You hear President Roosevelt's declaration of war. The news is terrifying, but you're glad that the United States is going to defend itself against this terrible attack.

You receive orders to remain at Pearl Harbor for now. There is talk that the Japanese might try to invade, so you will be needed here. The world has changed, and you don't know what will happen next. Nobody does.

THE END

To follow another path, turn to page 9.
To read the conclusion, turn to page 101.

"I'll stay," you say. "I can do just as much good here as I can at the hospital."

The doctor smiles. "Thank you," he says.

You work for hours. When you finally stop for a minute, something seems very odd. Then it hits you. It's quiet. There are no more bombs or explosions. You didn't even notice when the attack ended. You sink onto a chair, exhausted from the day. It's dusk. A weary nurse notices you and walks over.

"You've been such a great help," she says. "Why don't you go home and get some rest? There's still a lot of work to be done, and we'll need fresh nurses tomorrow."

You nod. A small boat is leaving for the shore, and you climb aboard. Soon, you're making your way toward home.

The battleships *Cassin* and *Downes* were destroyed.

In the fading light, you see the destruction all around you. Several battleships are still burning. Piles of twisted metal lie everywhere. It's hard to believe that anyone survived this attack. You realize that the United States can no longer stay out of this war. You're afraid, but you're determined to do your part for your country.

THE END

To follow another path, turn to page 9.
To read the conclusion, turn to page 101.

On December 8, 1941, President Franklin D. Roosevelt asked Congress to declare war on Japan.

CHAPTER 5

Remember Pearl Harbor

The attack on December 7, 1941, took the world by surprise. The attack began just before 8:00 in the morning. By 10:00, it was over. Before the attack, the United States was at peace, determined not to join the war in Europe. By the time the last Japanese bomber pilot flew away, everything had changed.

The next day, December 8, President Roosevelt delivered one of his most famous speeches. He called December 7, 1941, "a date which will live in infamy." He asked Congress to declare war on Japan. His request was granted.

By all accounts, the attack was a success for the Japanese. They crippled the U.S. Navy. In all, the Japanese sank or severely damaged 18 American ships. The Japanese destroyed 188 American aircraft and damaged 159 others. At least 2,400 Americans died.

On the other hand, the Japanese lost only 29 airplanes. Only 55 Japanese airmen were killed. They also lost five midget submarines. Of the 10 crewmen on the midget submarines, nine died. One was captured and held as a prisoner of war.

But the Japanese failed to destroy the three American aircraft carriers normally stationed at Pearl Harbor. USS *Enterprise* and USS *Lexington* were delivering planes to nearby islands. The third, USS *Saratoga*, had gone to San Diego for repairs.

In the coming months, all but three of the American ships damaged in the attack were repaired. Only *Arizona*, *Oklahoma*, and *Utah* were completely lost. In just a year, the U.S. fleet was back to its full strength.

The Pearl Harbor attack united the American people against Japan and the Axis powers. The United States joined with the Soviet Union, Great Britain, and other European countries to form the Allied forces. Together, they faced the huge Axis armies in both Europe and the South Pacific.

At home, Americans were afraid. Many cities enforced blackouts at night to avoid enemy bombing. Thousands of Japanese Americans on the West Coast were removed from their homes. They were forced to live in internment camps under the watchful eye of the government.

The sunken *Arizona* remains
at the bottom of Pearl Harbor
below the memorial.

In June 1942, the Battle of Midway in the Pacific Ocean was a turning point in the war. At that battle, U.S. forces defeated the Japanese Navy. From then on, the United States had the advantage. Japan never completely recovered its sea forces.

In August 1945, the United States dropped two atomic bombs on Japan. The first destroyed the city of Hiroshima. The second fell on the city of Nagasaki. Within weeks, the Japanese stopped fighting. The war was over.

Pearl Harbor is still an important military base due to its location in the Pacific Ocean. Almost from the day of the attack, people wanted to create a memorial to the people who died at Pearl Harbor. In 1962, former President Dwight Eisenhower dedicated the *Arizona* Memorial. It was built on the water above the wreckage of *Arizona*, which can still be seen today.

TIME LINE

September 1, 1939 — World War II begins.

September 27, 1940 — Germany, Italy, and Japan agree to form the Axis powers.

December 7, 1941

> **3:42 a.m.** — A Japanese submarine is spotted near Pearl Harbor.

> **6:15 a.m.** — The first wave of Japanese attackers heads to Oahu.

> **6:45 a.m.** — A Japanese submarine is sunk outside the entrance to Pearl Harbor.

> **7:15 a.m.** — The second attack wave takes off from Japanese aircraft carriers.

> **7:49 a.m.** — Commander Mitsuo Fuchida gives the signal to attack.

> **7:55 a.m.** — Telegraph operators on Ford Island send out the first reports of the attack.

> **8:01 a.m.** — *Oklahoma* and *West Virginia* are hit.

> **8:06 a.m.** — The first bomb hits *Arizona*.

> **8:10 a.m.** — *Arizona* is destroyed.

9:02 a.m. — The second wave of Japanese bombers attack Pearl Harbor.

9:27 a.m. — *Cassin* overturns onto *Downes*.

9:30 a.m. — *Shaw* explodes.

9:45 a.m. — Japanese planes begin returning to their aircraft carriers. The attack is over.

December 8, 1941 — The United States, Great Britain, and Canada declare war on Japan.

June 4–7, 1942 — American naval forces defeat Japan's fleet at the Battle of Midway.

February–March 1945 — The United States defeats Japanese forces at the Battle of Iwo Jima.

May 7, 1945 — Germany surrenders, ending World War II in Europe.

August 6, 1945 — The United States drops the first atomic bomb on the Japanese city of Hiroshima.

August 9, 1945 — The world's second atomic bomb destroys the Japanese city of Nagasaki.

August 14, 1945 — Japan agrees to surrender.

September 2, 1945 — Japanese officials sign the surrender document, officially ending World War II in the Pacific.

OTHER PATHS TO EXPLORE

In this book, you've seen how the events experienced at Pearl Harbor on December 7, 1941, look different from three points of view.

Perspectives on history are as varied as the people who lived it. You can explore other paths on your own to learn more about what happened. Seeing history from many points of view is an important part of understanding it.

Here are some ideas for other Pearl Harbor attack points of view to explore:

- ♦ A few American fighter pilots were able to take off during the attack. What was it like to take on the Japanese fighter planes in the sky?

- ♦ More than 80 civilians were killed or injured during the attack. What would it have been like to live in Honolulu or nearby cities during the attack?

- ♦ Before the attack, Japan launched five midget submarines toward Pearl Harbor. Each vessel carried two men each. Only one of the men survived. What would it have been like to try to sneak into Pearl Harbor aboard a small submarine?

READ MORE

Hanel, Rachael. *The Japanese American Internment: An Interactive History Adventure.* Mankato, Minn.: Capstone Press, 2008.

Sutcliffe, Jane. *The Attack on Pearl Harbor.* Mankato, Minn.: Capstone Press, 2006.

White, Steve. *The Battle of Midway: The Destruction of the Japanese Fleet.* New York: Rosen, 2007.

Whiting, Jim. *The Story of the Attack on Pearl Harbor.* Hockessin, Del.: Mitchell Lane, 2006.

INTERNET SITES

FactHound offers a safe, fun way to find Internet sites related to this book. All of the sites on FactHound have been researched by our staff.

Here's how:
1. Visit *www.facthound.com*
2. Choose your grade level.
3. Type in this book ID **1429620102** for age-appropriate sites. You may also browse subjects by clicking on letters, or by clicking on pictures and words.
4. Click on the **Fetch It** button.

FactHound will fetch the best sites for you!

GLOSSARY

admiral (AD-muh-ruhl) — an officer in the navy with a rank higher than that of captain

ammunition (am-yuh-NISH-uhn) — bullets and other objects that can be fired from weapons

commander (kuh-MAN-duhr) — a person who leads a group of people in the armed forces

debris (duh-BREE) — the scattered pieces of something that has been broken or destroyed

fleet (FLEET) — a group of warships under one command

hatch (HACH) — a covered hole in a floor, deck, door, wall, or ceiling

medic (MED-ik) — a soldier trained to give medical help in an emergency or during a battle

military (MIL-uh-ter-ee) — the armed forces of a country

torpedo (tor-PEE-doh) — an underwater weapon that explodes when it hits a target, such as a ship

turret (TUR-it) — a rotating part on top of a ship or military vehicle that holds a weapon

BIBLIOGRAPHY

Carlisle, Rodney P., ed. *One Day in History —
December 7, 1941.* New York: Collins, 2006.

Kimmett, Larry, and Margaret Regis. *The Attack
on Pearl Harbor: An Illustrated History.* Seattle:
Navigator, 1991.

La Forte, Robert S., and Ronald E. Marcello, eds.
*Remembering Pearl Harbor: Eyewitness Accounts by
U.S. Military Men and Women.* Wilmington, Del.:
SR Books, 1991.

Layton, Edwin T. *"And I Was There": Pearl Harbor
and Midway — Breaking the Secrets.* New York:
W. Morrow, 1985.

Pearl Harbor Attack: Index of Action Reports
http://www.history.navy.mil/faqs/faq66-4.htm

Pearl Harbor Navy Medical Activities
http://www.history.navy.mil/faqs/faq66-5.htm

Prange, Gordon William. *At Dawn We Slept:
The Untold Story of Pearl Harbor.* New York:
McGraw-Hill, 1981.

Prange, Gordon William. *God's Samurai: Lead Pilot
at Pearl Harbor.* Washington: Brassey's, 1990.

Worth, Roland H. *Pearl Harbor: Selected Testimonies,
Fully Indexed, from the Congressional Hearings
(1945–1946) and Prior Investigations of the Events
Leading Up to the Attack.* Jefferson, N.C.: McFarland
and Co., 1993.

INDEX